G000154391

ABOUT THE AUTHOR

Kathy Pimlott's debut pamphlet *Goose Fair Night* was published by
The Emma Press in 2016, followed by *Elastic Glue* in 2019. Her work has
appeared in many magazines and anthologies.

Kathy was born and raised in Nottingham but has spent her adult life in
London, the last 45 or so years in Covent Garden, specifically Seven Dials,
home of the broadsheet and the ballad. She has been a barmaid, social
worker and community activist, sold pre-revolutionary Chinese art and
jewellery, worked on a political and financial risk journal, in arts
television, in cross-disciplinary artist development and in conservation in
the public realm. She makes a lot of jam.

http://www.kathypimlott.co.uk

Kathy Pimlott
the small manoeuvres

VERVE
POETRY PRESS
BIRMINGHAM

PUBLISHED BY VERVE POETRY PRESS
https://vervepoetrypress.com
mail@vervepoetrypress.com

All rights reserved
© 2022 Kathy Pimlott

The right of Kathy Pimlott to be identified as author of this work has been
asserted in accordance with section 77 of the Copyright, Designs and
Patents Act 1988.

No part of this work may be reproduced, stored or transmitted in any form
or by any means, graphic, electronic, recorded or mechanical, without the
prior written permission of the publisher.

FIRST PUBLISHED APR 2022

Printed and bound in the UK
by ImprintDigital, Exeter

ISBN: 978-1-913917-05-0

Cover illustration by Sharon Smart
www.sharonsmart.com

For Ella and Eliza

i.m. Robert Pimlott (1953-2021)

CONTENTS

Acknowledgements

the small manoeuvres

Overlooked

If you go upstairs to the second floor
of the record shop where they keep
those niche recordings, zydeco, hi-life,
which you might in this empty moment
be revisiting like a lost love or trawling
for novelty to spike your jaded heart,
if you look out the window, not the one
that gives onto what, until just yesterday,
was Angels, costumier to the stars,
but the other, you'll see into a kitchen,
its pans, its colander and graded sieves
hanging like a half-curtain and, beyond,
which you won't see but must imagine,
one ripe banana balanced on a hand
of greener fruits, lending encouragement
by way of ethylene. And look, a woman,
older, white-haired, is dancing alone,
her still-lithe wrists held high and snaky.
Then, because her unknown music ends,
she opens her eyes, sees you looking
and, instead of ducking quickly out of sight,
looks right back, smiling, stares you down.

Revelations

There's a vertical track in the cushiony flesh of my left lobe,
where a looked-after child on my lap caught and dragged,
not meaning to, a gold hoop to rest deep down. For months
I was lop-sided until I summoned the nerve to ease the ring
from its softly bedded place and leave my ears forever naked.

All my scars are ridiculous: negligible traces of mishaps,
like the sickle on my index finger memorialising the waste
of a whole block of White Stilton cheese at a time when
it mattered, the slipped knife having conjured such
a startling amount of blood; or the perfectly round dent

bored in my left knee from when I misjudged my jump
over the garden rake I'd convinced a cousin would do
for a skipping rope; or the silver thread in the cross-hatch
on my right hand from the night I missed a step in the dark
of a poetry cellar and fell on a glass I hadn't had a sip from,

painlessly severing the tendon which operates the thumb.
It was fished down with something like a crochet hook,
reattached as though I was a pot doll whose rubber bands
had perished. I imagine there's a scar from the cut when I had
no push at all left in me but that's private, even I can't see it.

So you know

Some people, riddled with slivers left in in case removal
elicits a geyser of blood, hurt in intricate, outlandish ways,
hung with fetishes. Some compromise at the wrong time.

Others are beaten with wooden spoons, sprayed with words
cheap and corrosive as One Shot. Some are invaded
but I, I dodged it all. Hoo-ha and to-do make me twitchy.

I swallowed that unforgiving adage, 'I used to feel
hard done by having no shoes until I met a man with no feet'.
And, reader, I met him, scooting along on a proto-skateboard,

all torso and leather gauntlets. Or it's a gift of levitation,
to hover inches above the scene, being both there and here.
Or I could say it's generational. Just get on and work.

My tears are fatal to others so you must allow me obliqueness.
I've entertained sorrow but now I think it's a bird trapped
in a room, contagious panic solved by opening a window,

followed by a dustpan and brush. Given my general lack of threat,
I may appear kind but I'm conserving energy. Understanding
undoes me. What matters now is grace on a wire, enough sleep.

The Baby in the Wardrobe

Do you remember the story of the baby in the wardrobe,
its desiccated body wrapped in newspaper? How the baby
was decades old but the newspaper was last week's edition?

This is my story. The baby is dead but I bring it fresh news,
re-wrap it in editorials, ads, crosswords with undiminished
tenderness, newsprint smudging my attentive fingertips.

I'm not trying to reanimate the baby with another bomb
or preposterous scandal, I'm just not ready to dispose of it,
though it's no use, something of a liability if truth be told

and it's pure fortune there's no odour, pure fortune.
Another thing about the wardrobe baby is how I was the baby
for a long time, until this body grew, enclosing baby-me.

How did the baby die? Was it stifled, done to death
because it cried and cried? I think it was abandoned
(though not quite, for here its brittle little body is) because

it wasn't interesting. Some think all babies can be someone,
Jesus or Astaire say, that conviction of grace. But let's be honest,
all that crying makes it nigh on impossible to get any work done.

Small Hours

In one of the many ways I'm guilty,
I cursed my baby to a life of broken sleep,
laying my hand on her back, lovingly
rousing her to check she was still alive.

Now when I creep in in the dark to feel
her breathing on the back of my hand,
my mother stirs from her merciful sleep,
asks what time it is. For when I'm not here,

which is mostly, I bought a special clock:
press once to hear the time and once again
for day and date. But tonight I am, carry
her hearing aids to their cradle to charge.

One buzzes on my palm and I think I hear
a faraway voice, an urgent message
just out of earshot. Now that she can see
nothing by looking, all the looking things

are done with, leaving only the voices
of talking books, their complicated family
crochet work, sagas of poor girls' privations
bravely overcome and a clock saying 3.45am.

As you are 93, I must be 68

Something is wrong with the guttering.
It could be nests. This is one problem.

Another is the rockery nearly overrun
by creeping jenny and oak saplings

which would become a forest if left
to their own devices and the heathers

which promised well have disappeared
and someone stole the lilies-of-the-valley.

This world is both wilder and straitened,
like the bins. It's never the right rubbish

at the right time. Roses from the garden
blow petal by petal onto polished wood.

Shop roses just nod over. We'd like to be
the first kind. Who knows what will upset

the system? Today it's eggs. Yesterday
eggs were fine. The body is after all

a capricious toddler, prone to sudden
and alarming rebellions. It's impossible

and the cat's a mixed blessing, flinches
but sleeps exactly where you want your feet.

No-one knows what to buy you. It's all
hand cream or orchids, a plant not naturally

companionable. We talk about memories,
what remains and why, like the day the house

filled with crane flies, wispy legs dangling,
or that green two-piece and boater, elastic

tight under my chin; how, finding an old snap,
you remembered the colour of your frock

but not the six camels behind you, gravely
processing along the stony Kentish beach.

The fridge has taken to defrosting itself,
invisible shallow pools on its glass shelves.

No-one knows the cat's age, what happened
before she came. Once, you and your friend

set fire to a rival's coat. I had fun with drugs.
Now it would seem we're both old women.

Tripping

I won't say 'fall', as in 'I had a fall', with all the flaky crust
that clings around that phrase, a dandruff of declining years.

Not yet. Instead, I'll say 'a trip', recall how in a summer field
I started to dissolve into the buzzing fabric of a blissful world,

was gone to the elbow before l said, aloud I think, my mouth
a stranger to me, 'No, not yet'. Despite that teeth-edge race,

the just-about-to vertigo, I had a choice and chose no, not yet.
Now, tidy with the totems I've accrued, passes, grandchildren,

silver gravitas, I'm toppled by an incontestable 'Yes, right now'
I can't resist, ending not in Nirvana but in an ambulance.

The 41st anniversary present

First thought had been a bunch of sweet peas off the plot,
loose and loud as girls after school. Second thought,
and full marks for bagging a bargain, three carnivores.

The labels don't give their botanical names but do say
'not for human consumption.' Unnecessary. Only Barry
has any bulk and his liver/scrotum cross, his veiny-ness

require no warning-off. Carmel is the one who works,
patrols the window to snag small storm flies in her hair.
I place her touching the glass as the flies don't fly as such,

just jitter around. Barry and Cyril who, it turns out,
are really only for show, relax in their hot tub on the sill.
Now and again, though I know I shouldn't, I poke Cyril

to see if his labia dentata traps still work and they do,
languidly. Barry's an enigma. His felty chalices could
be full of flies but I don't care to ferret around in there.

What it's like

It's one of those wooden boxes on four legs.
On either side of the carrying handle,
three tiers of shallow trays fold out in steps,

one half-tier adrift, its struts come loose.
I don't remember if I bought it or was it a gift?
Me picturing myself, head bent, under lamplight

or someone's kind encouragement? Either way,
it's full of stuff: long skeins of faded silks
from a brief passion for embroidery,

as much to do with the grace of my hands
rising and falling at the frame as anything.
Some silks are still banded and tidy,

others tangled beyond undoing from single strands
pulled out without first cutting a length.
Tissue patterns, blue outlines, wrap round spools

of silver thread from my mandala phase –
such aspirations, so little patience, aptitude.
Sequins languish, untroubled by needles.

Jaunty rick-rack braid, acquired from my mother,
snags in scissors long dull enough for children
whose orderly name tapes tumble, frayed and free.

These buttons cut from the inside seams of jackets
or pearly, saved from matinee coats, tell hard tales.
Most ambitious of all – the intractable zips. It's like that.

Advice to the daughters

I believe I've drawn my knees up to my chest
for enough reasons to be allowed to advise.

I've courted death in back lanes, gathered up
sheets to cover my nakedness, waited to see

if the combat veterans and workaday crazy boys
would leave me intact. I've failed my driving test;

finally acknowledged the truth of that last report –
I do indeed lack the humility of a true scholar,

have squandered the fleeting hour on tv and notions.
Freshly-stitched, I've hopped off the high hard bed

to smoke furiously in a day-room, a voice in my ear
narrating the terrible life-cycle of salmon. Wrists silted

heavy with lack of sleep, I've realised the true extent
of my affections, their uselessness, ruining each high-day

with a newsflash of your sudden and banal deaths. Surely
enough teeth have fallen away for me to claim wisdom?

Listen, we're here because we're here, but that's by-the-by,
what I'm saying is, at all times, earn your own living.

Residential Social Work, Grade 1

I used to look after special children
washed up into the care of uncertificated drifters,
like me, who hadn't mapped a career,

lived with them in their big house,
wiped noses, zipped up coats,
held them on my lap in the lino-ed TV room,
let them stroke my face and hair.

We'd sing in the minibus, Blue is the Colour
or Yellow Submarine and twice a year visit
the shoe shop kept open for us after tea,
replacing tan sandals with the same again
but bigger.

On birthdays and just before Christmas,
I'd stand to the side as visiting families
floundered, atoning with chocolate.

Back then I read that special children like these
were mighty wizards re-born into a hell
of half-remembered spells, magic gestures
drained of power.

The world has changed. They'll all be dead by now,
Marcus, Juliet, Hugo, Julia, Graham, Steven, Jenny,
Benny, Bubba Lee, with their susceptible chests,
faulty hearts. I'm not who I was.

Grand Union Canal Adventure

We three old girls, fractured
by the usual losses, aren't mended
Japanese-style with precious seams
that make each fissure sing,
but rivetted: serviceable, not art.

To prove our mettle, we choose
to chug along the old Grand Union,
moor by fields of roosting geese
to sway in darkness on the water's
shallow, dreamless shift.

Forty feet above the Ouse, I'm left.
The others go below to show me
I can, despite my doubts, skipper us
along the strait way of the aqueduct,
not falter, step back into empty air

down into the river's wilder waters.
On a narrow boat there's no choice
but to make the small manoeuvres
that trundle us over the drop and on,
now and again to know the satisfaction

of a perfect approach to a bend.
Shins bruised, knuckles scraped raw,
we tie up, step ashore to climb the hill
up to the Peace Pagoda, so golden,
so unlikely, outside Milton Keynes.

'So Bracing!'

Skegness and his sisters, Mablethorpe and Chapel,
smell of ripe drainage channels segmenting land
that shrugs to dunes, slumps into beach, now sand,
now mud, to a far sea's silver, all ridge and ripple.

Or the tide's in and you wade out miles to swim,
belly grazing the sea bed, costume fat with silt,
return, blue-lipped and dithering to towels' grit.
Marram deepens your heart line, slices your palm.

At night in caravans, wind-burn and salt-burn flare.
Spat-on hanky hems are twisted to tease grains
from crannies. The sands are empty, just remains
of castles' torn paper flags mark you were there

dancing on coils of lugworm casts, sea-bleached,
teasing crabs on the no-nonsense pleasure beach.

Return to the Terminus

Too often now I sway into the night,
that cosy winter dark between tea and
the turning out of pubs and cinemas,
a late traveller fogging a rattling bus.
See me on the upper deck with the dogs
and other coughers, taken up with smoking
in that sophisticated way, dragon-nostrils.

I shouldn't keep going back, am already yellow
beyond scrubbing. These comfortable excursions
just won't do while all the while life howls
for attention. Last year a clever man I knew
a bit, courted a death he didn't believe in.
Visiting, face it, out of a desire to be blessed,
by happenstance I was invited into the scan,

into the intimacy of his scarred insides,
to witness a death sentence, 90% sure, but, ah,
that golden 10. First question: can I still
have a drink? He died, swollen, in a hard clutch.
And now this other man, mine, heads that way too.
But anyhow, look, here comes the whipsmart clippie
machine grazing her hip, its crank and buttons

primed for pernickety fares. Only she commands
the bell: one for stop, two sharp dings for go.
If I don't tell you, how will you ever know about
that bronco ride of side benches, the fear of slipping
right off the bus as the driver speeds, skips stops, reckless
on corners, to the end of his shift? It's late, so join me,
grip the pole, lean out into those bright, melancholy lights.

Snap

All week we trail the beach photographer,
you in your sister's hand-me-down costume,
me in exemplary white underwear, posing
until he snaps us, two bold girls on the sands.
I am sturdy. You are pale. The state of our hair
betrays our differences. I have no sister yet
while yours jives with every swinging door.

My dad's a tall salesman, yours a gaunt joiner,
never recovered from that mysterious year
in a Japanese camp, bets, they say, to forget.
Sometimes you don't even have furniture or chips,
just bread sprinkled with vinegar, while we have

jam on our Yorkshire puddings, and scatter cushions,
each shaped like one of the suits in a pack of cards.

Entertaining Sammy Davis Jnr
in St Ives, 1962

On a Sunday, the amusement arcade in the harbour
is closed but I say to the fisherman/machine-minder,
'Look, just this once, while the Sally Army's in full toot
on the slipway, open up the back and let us in. It's Sammy,
he's getting nervous. He needs a casino milieu'. And Matty,
though fearful of reprisals from the Methodists and God,
lets us in. Now Sammy leans against the Penny Falls
and sighs, semi-content and nearly soothed, his clicking finger
softly brushing the pad of his thumb, his blind eye bright.

A Run Out to Zennor

There are three things about the Tinner's Arms:
firstly, the extra blue waxed twist of salt
in the bag of crisps that time; second, how bats

appeared out of the gloam, skimming our hair
when, bored of adults, we took the sunken path
to the cliff, how we screamed back to safety,

to the bench-and-table combos bleached by rains,
to yellow lights, our paper straws chewed flat
in empty Vimto bottles; third, Morveren

luring Mathey Trewella with her song.
How they dwelt, him blue-lipped, her all muscle,
down among black rocks where barnacles cling,

living on jelly anemones, silver darlings.
A fourth thing I learned later was DH Lawrence,
newly-wed, mouthing off against the War

and Frieda, a Richthofen, signalling to subs
they said and ordered out. But the thing now
is the cliff walk back from Zennor to Man's Head,

the spring of tough grass, dog-faced seals
breaking a restive grid of wind across light
across eddys past Wicca Pool, Mussel Point,

Carn Naun, Pen Enys Point. And later still
I find it was, in fact, Mathey's strong tenor
captured Morveren, that she dragged herself,

wet and weed-draped, up to St Senara,
how the good folk drove the love-struck pair,
man and fishy girl, back down and out to sea.

Three men in a pub, probably, they made it happen

We'd been deep country for more than a week, grown mossy,
credulous, almost religious, craved spectacle. So when we saw
the poster in the closed shop window and another, wind-ripped

on a gatepost down the lane, we were hooked. What did we expect?
We conjured up trebuchet or cannon with a sexy, gleeful shame.
Bob said a big kite, artistic and skilful in its way but, nonetheless,

it would be a disappointment. Parachute? There was so much room
for interpretation. Anticipation was a fever. At the advertised time
we went to the field as instructed, paid the man and stood around.

City-spoilt to the core, we began to get fidgety, until a Luton
arrived, dropped a side, revealing shelves of lurid pop,
confectionery and bagged snacks and, in its own sweet time,

a little frayed and muddy, the event was assembled. We bought
five raffle tickets, a loving spoon, hot doughnuts, won shampoo
on the bottle stall. Time ticked on and out of things to buy

we faltered, wondered whether we should call it a day, admit
we'd been foolish. And then we heard the helicopter's winnow,
low enough to whip the bunting round the van, make dogs bark.

Above our raised faces, it circled the field in that tilted way,
dangling – white, weighty, on a line – The Flying Pig. Was it dead?
Alive? Which was more thrilling? The best thing we had ever seen.

Limelight

This silverfish, a comma on the mastic
which joins the lino and the skirting board

wants only but keenly to find a crevice
and disappear into its damp obscurity,

escape light cast into the bathroom
from the windows of the shop across the road.

If it must be seen it wants to be glimpsed
as a floater, perhaps a vitreous flicker.

The silverfish eschews limelight. I foil
its sugar quest. It finds a crack and vanishes.

Pests

I poison mice because they come indoors
through hollow walls where gas and water pipes
and tv cables breach the plasterboard,
though wire wool's jammed into the smallest gaps.

They love indoors where there's so much to eat:
old photographs, used tissues, flakes of skin,
crust crumbs from a carelessly torn baguette,
those dinner scrapings that just missed the bin.

I can't abide their sly periphery dash,
their droppings peppering jam and pickle jars
and, worst of all, the thing that creeps my flesh,
their whispering among the swaddled pears.

I choose to put my ease above their lives.
It must be poison. Mice don't compromise.

Some Context in Mitigation

We like to know when our next meal's coming,
what it'll be, think about tea as we're dishing up
dinner, know pork's superior to beef, how to hide

the crackling for later. We say adding herbs
is mucking about with good food, make gravy
properly, from a packet. Our lips are puckered

not from smoking but from judging, one step away
from the abyss. We exchange glances when a woman
laughs loudly, are quick to spot a lack of knickers

under a rabbit coat. If we'd had regression therapy,
which we didn't because we didn't have time
to be depressed, we wouldn't have been Cleopatra

or an alchemist. No, we'd stretch back through years,
a line of getters-on-with-it and though we're short
of artists and activists, there is the one who stabbed

her husband with the sewing scissors and got shipped
to the back of beyond; one who fled to Cornwall
on account of Daphne du Maurier and the change;

and even fearful Enid once went for Alfred's throat
with the edge of a white-hot frying pan, because,
because she just couldn't be doing with it any more.

After the Fall

So when a manhole cover flips,
drops me down, scraped and shaken,
though only five, I pause to consider

if now is a suitable time to shout *Help!*
like in the stories, attract attention
by waving my red cardy or whether

that would be showing off and
I should stand quietly in the drain
until someone notices I'm gone.

Savings

Thinking of Eliot who was himself thinking of Dante,
I remark on the throng on Bridlesmith Gate, undone
by Christmas shopping. You say, as throng as Throp's wife
when she hung herself with the dishclout. I think hanged,
say you make them up, but it's years of little enough
– a rasher of wind and a fried snowball – that sets you
to concertina old print into spills to light a fire, coax
red-gold in caves of slack. What's in your bag?
Shim shams for ducks to waddle up.

> This is the lore that keeps death at bay:
> never do washing on New Year's Day.

> This is the lore that keeps death at bay:
> never cut toenails on New Year's Day.

The lore crowds in like cold at your back and it sounds
like Billy Ball's taproom. And though these coddled days
like as not you're sweating cobs, part of you (your clack,
your tabs?) is wistful for that chilly realm of simple boys
and calipered girls and, piggling at nostalgia, pines for
the plain-faced comfort of a shelf with separate tins
for rent, for coal, the Pru, your bury money.

Apprentice Pattern Cutter

For Jo

She's trapped by women who can put on
their lipstick without a mirror, answer back
full of chelp, while she is fourteen and knows
nothing. Toilet breaks are timed but this is a way
towards some glamour – like in the pictures,

where women lounge in swaying marabou.
The Kathleens, Dollies, Dots, with swollen feet,
deft hands above the drop feed, zip along
a double French seam, set a sleeve just right
and there's magic in that. She shakes out cloth,

spreads it, makes a snip and rips across
the warp. With tailors' chalk, she snicks darts,
cuts notches to match so collars sit flat
on collar bones. Bent forward, wielding both
plain and pinking shears, her wrist soon sports

a ganglion. Hers is a world of pins stuck in
and forgotten, of bias cut, stretch and pucker,
of slip or bulk jamming under the needle.
From eight till six she cuts out evening blouses,
walks home to save the fare for velvet gloves,

a fold of voile hidden in her bag. She dreams
of devoré, guipure, silk charmeuse, sleeping,
measures yards from nose to fingertip,
the fabric's drop brushing her pretty feet:
picqué, organza, crêpe de Chine, georgette.

Five Unusual Things

You open the quarter-lights, get out of the car.
'Five minutes' you say 'and while I'm gone,

look for five unusual things.' And I'm alone
on a back street of workshops and offices.

No-one appears. There are no balloons,
no burglaries. Nothing disturbs the street.

Two thirds up the warehouse wall
the brick course swivels ninety degrees,

three fanciful rows and then back
to a sensible horizontal. I breathe

on the window, draw a face that fades
with the clearing mist, breathe again

and it reappears. Years later,
when you've been gone forever,

clocking a sign for invisible menders, I say
for you, 'you don't see many of those.'

Enid and Me

Old people shouldn't sleep
with the young you say,
it drains their vigour.
You give me a whisky sting

in tea-tinged milk to counter sleet,
a thimble of port before school
for my blood, while you'll take
only a Christmas Snowball.

Asked at the right time
you'll open your mouth,
let your glossy dentures slip
to show where a tipsy dentist

took out all your teeth to save you
the expense of future decay.
Mistress of madeira, piccalilli,
the scotch egg, you teach me

to coax butter between paddles
into dainty curls. The grownups will
be lively, drunk and playing Peggy Lee,
while upstairs, we'll have the story

of your dash with a bowl on pig-killing day,
of how you fainted under the cane.
You tell me about bombed bodies
stacked in the swimming baths,

your mam's red hair, long enough
to sit on, how the doctor made her
cut it off to cure her headaches.
At *The Ten Commandments*

we leave before the end (but after
the Parting of the Red Sea) to make tea.
It's not all old times. Once, you make
a pineapple sponge from a book.

Close-Ups in Lockdown

Confined to the same streets, I glean details,
snap the gilded bas reliefs of parish arms
on lamp-posts, benches on the Embankment
changing from duck to sphinx to camel going east.

Looking up I've caught cupolas, Justice, Art,
Geometry, both draped and nude, old wars'
bronze memorials and, in front of palaces,
arcs of wallflowers edging tulips going over.

The finely-crafted wrought iron gates
and grilles of our secret powerful and rich
have been revelatory, their curlicues
and spikes a refinement of exclusion.

I've captured Clement Danes' electric bells
bouncing childhood rhymes around the Aldwych
but spared you abandoned restaurants,
their dried-up skimmia in forsaken troughs.

I've skipped all the shop windows blinded
with chipboard, promises to be back soon,
to focus on once-neglected things, distract
a fretting heart which doesn't know what's next.

Look, here's a letterbox, deco, and another,
arts & crafts. Draw comfort from these apertures,
so elegantly dressed for bills, news, billets doux,
when all you love are elsewhere, out of reach.

She Longs for Breakfast with Dolly and Arthur

Last night, late, I ate one of the miniature cartons
of cereal from your Variety Pack in the cupboard.
These days, when distance is a moral obligation
and no-one knows when we'll eat together again,
I think of that hot summer morning and you two,
topless at the table, working your way through
a five-course breakfast as we discuss vampires'
cosmetic choices, how trees talk root to root,
the invention of seconds, minutes, hours, days
and months, which cereal is the most grown up.
Last night, solitary, sad, I chose Rice Krispies,
listened for their snap, crackle, pop. I worry
very soon we'll be too old for this dear nonsense.

Regent's Park, April 2020

Then I thought I heard a lion's roar, a command
to surrender. But all I could see was cow parsley
lapping the legs of silver birches, an ice house
overtaken by ivy. All flights grounded, birdsong
was flooding the quiet – chinking, fluid, making
a wonder of the midweek. A green woodpecker
laughed from above. I couldn't see him but knew
he was there. Hemmed in, fancy seeks out cracks
which give onto savannah. It's not unreasonable
to think I heard a lion, or perhaps it was a tiger.

Site of Special Scientific Interest

The island has been left to dormice, foxes, hives
and the water plant. An old Peace sprawls,
flushing yellow to pink. The rest has gone over.
Across the bridge it's biblical: plagues lay waste
to fruit and crucifers and just when you thought
you'd escaped, a wet spell incubates late blight.

Mice spoil apples, roll spent whisky bottles
across shed floors. Enthusiasms flare
then gutter, pricey secateurs are left
among the raspberry canes and drums
of half-steeped comfrey sludge reek brown.
Each season brings new immolations, strokes.

Someone broke into Reg's shed, made off
with a strimmer, several tins of soup. I think
of them gingerly tilting their bowls. In the event
of a Complete Breakdown we'll almost certainly
get a gun. Chicken Jim has one, thinks he's the boss
but he no longer has chickens, foxes got them all.

Borlotti always do well, their wine-freckled beans
the eggs of a very small bird. There's talk
of fixing Easter which would make potato planting
easier. No-one now uses their bare arse to test
the soil's warmth. Mine is pricked by sea holly
as I squat behind bushes, see cubs in the clearing.

City, first-floor maisonette, patio

Ours is a cockeyed habitat, wind
whipped loco by high rise, a July
heat simmering up on applause
from the theatre underneath us.

A barrel of caught rain run-off
fosters our very own mosquitos.
Each leaf strains towards light
rationed by brute intersections

where the heavens hide and peep.
We plant geraniums, fuchsias, herbs
in plastic troughs. Soil grows sour.
Thyme, too overlooked, rosemary,

waterlogged, shrink back, give up
and crisp to brown. This day is grey
but a bright beak, a coral flower,
tenacious, bold and metropolitan

above the dust of Victorian ferns,
sing out and the Lenten rose, staked
but still down-faced, glows green.
The pavers are muddy with earth

turned by ordinary birds who
drop in for bugs and the fatballs
hung from the Norfolk Island Pine.
It shouldn't be here, the curious

pentagon planes of its many floors
reaching, what? thirty feet? passing
our bedroom window, the upstairs flat,
to prove we can, we do, grow trees.

Seven Dials: The Rookery Redux

The rain collects by drains stopped up
with fatbergs from the eateries,
in cracks and trips of paving stones
and setts lifted and re-laid. Step carelessly

and soak your shoes. Do you belong here?
Do you loop grey nets to foil
the suck and growl of traffic's heat?
Do you open your windows at all?

At night the seven streets pinball
each drunk chorus, each deal undone.
Roused sleepers turn and mutter
vows to flee to Harpenden,

Peterborough, somewhere normal.
Money's what it's always been about,
this star conceived for profit,
more rental by the frontage foot

than that for squares. Cute schemes
leap and crash, leave logos,
hidden eglomise, blind windows.
The crack crowd keeps its ground, Soho

to St Giles, between cameras and lights.
Watchful, loose-jointed, urgent,
heads over cupped palm, with sudden
limping dashes, they feint,

twist and turn, wry faced and pissen pants,
hopeless and eternally hunting
for that one good deal among the pop-ups,
the fairy-lit trees, the bunting.

They count on you getting tired, giving up

No-one lives here, you'd think, in the city's glitzy heart
except the agile young wanting to shimmy and shine
before taking a van out to somewhere more... private.

Yet here we are, in infill blocks we made them build
all those years ago, knowing the mums, the kids
since before they had their own, so close we hear

each other's sneezes, dying. Upstairs, temporary men
keep Spanish hours that clatter on their wooden floor,
my bedroom ceiling. They'll go. I know who plays away,

who cooks mackerel, who's been inside, uses Economy 7,
tunes in to Magic Radio. I know we're on borrowed time.
Where are the old girls of the market, theatres, print?

Gone to Guinnesses in the sky. Money wants no-one
to belong here, just pass through, hold no memories
worth fighting for to temper plans to squeeze the streets,

trick them out in shoddy to look like style, smell like profit.
Silly us. All that time we thought it ours, rallied, witnessed,
held the line, all that grief, just making it nice for Money.

Some Horses

Today the Household Cavalry came by on seven handsome bays,
each with a white blaze, slipping on the multi-coloured setts
past Chick 'n' Sours and Udderlicious, lost I think and laughing
in the morning rain. Last night it was two boys on skate boards.
Boys I say but old enough for scant beards, to know better,
clattering across the chamfered ledge of Orcs Nest, a raw rattle
in the empty street. I shouted them off with children sleeping.

There are no children sleeping. Two police horses pass just now
at a self-conscious clop. Someone who knows these things
told me the Strand Palace Hotel is full of military at present,
though couldn't say why. When we first moved in here
a troop of well-fed horses came by each morning, at halter,
down Shaftesbury Avenue, from stable to parade ground.
We'd open the window to get the full glory of their noise.

And there was that mid-afternoon, just after the poll tax riot.
I was working for a festival, holed up in the Market office
when police cantered through the arcades, scattering tourists
who shrank into shop doorways. You came to riding late,
the girls on ponies, you on giant Drummer. It's a good story
you got a caution for galloping uphill in Richmond Park,
funny, but what would happen if we all broke the rules?

Weathers in the City

Our lead-laced down draughts gust
between high-rises, blow sex cards
from phone kiosks, shake plane trees
to sneezes. Not true winds as such.

Very rarely, a small dry frost or snow
will sit on rubbish sacks, out-of-town
van roofs or a still-flowering geranium,
to deliver one day of lovely hysteria

before slumping to grey inconvenience.
Or the old sun asserts itself, sets fires
in the fancy-angled glass of the City,
melting wing mirrors until, cooling,

it slinks off, faintly ridiculous. Without
oceans, rippling cornfields, crags,
we must find the sublime where we can.
Once, from the Lyric Hammersmith bar,

disappointed with the play, I looked out
and saw a triple rainbow, so clear it made
anything possible. And sometimes grubby air
rests on our cheeks as if we are loveable.

New Year

Everything is about to be destroyed – your people,
the great tits so busy about their little adjustments,

blackbirds, solitary robin, that imbecile of a fat pigeon,
all your allotted fauna doomed and, Lordy, you yourself

kill mice. But you can't just check out, pop yourself
into the chest freezer, bank on remaining undiscovered

until the sting has gone out of your odd disappearance.
Besides, today the sun shines, shaming you with the grime

on your windows. Your grandchildren will lead you home
from The Market, birds are bobbing away on the feeders

and the old tête-à-tête bulbs make their green effort again.
Who knows? Maybe this is the year we behave better.

Going to the Algerian Coffee Store:
500g Esotico

After the bin lorry has exhausted its beautifully modulated warnings,
after the glass lorry has shifted shingle, I step out into West Street

and the dog-end of last night, where a sweeper leans on his cart
and chats with his own country and a man with his trousers down

round his knees hobbles past, trailing a sleeping bag over his arm
like a negligent debutante with her stole. The pavements are tacky,

no loitering snappers, no witless number plates outside The Ivy yet,
just yellow drums of spent oil and bags of yesterday's fancy breads

awaiting their special collections under the heritage lamppost.
In what passes for peace, helicopters and gulls are still roosting

as I skirt the grim lieutenants outside Le Beaujolais, their hybrid engine
purring as they wait for lowly envoys on stolen bikes. My age exactly,

The Mousetrap sleeps the sleep of the utterly justified. Or, I leave
by the front onto Earlham Street, its hat stall, cinnamon and falafel fug,

risk an erratic rickshaw bike's right turn, cross the Circus, passing
the latest sensation at The Palace, into Soho's loud and narrow scuzz

of £12 haircuts, tattooists, Aladdin, leather masks, the endless churn
of fit outs. And all the boys, visitors, the louche remains of glory days

drink coffee on Old Compton Street, study each other side-eyed across
the blue recycling bags and natty dogs. The choice of pastries is infinite.

Berwick Street Market, Mon Amour

Ian the Fish and the pink and white poultry man
and even, once, (ding dong!) that Leslie Phillips
browsing farmed trout and scallops, as though
he ever cooked, were effortlessly the thing, but now
it's all foil trays for one, those niche intolerances,
confected bonhomie, no melancholy, no arse.

The poultry man, so neatly trussed in his apron strings,
plump as a ballotine, complexion of a Medici cherub,
would probe his cheek with his wicked little tongue
as he gutted chicken, chicken, chicken, fat fingers
in the cavities, pulling down innards, setting aside
livers and tiny hearts. Who knows what became of him?

Ian was felled, first his mother-in-law and then his wife
within the month, and the shine just went off everything.
Mackerel, red mullet, sardines, eyes dulled, began to smell
of fish, which is always a bad sign. And that young man
with the lion's mane, stacks and flares, the David Bailey
of cauliflower and beetroot, took his truly artistic flash

to Knightsbridge on a promise of glamour and got lost.
Even the bit players, the real fur hat who shot on Sundays
and the huge man-boy in floppy shorts, the type who could
be needled into playing muscle for a pony, were sounder.
All swept away. Leslie Phillips carries on but hasn't been seen,
at least not by me, ogling the burritos and vegan Bratwurst.

Amsterdam

I exchanged one city for another, the smell of wisteria
everywhere. Flowers – even peonies – were so reasonable.

On King's Day the bridges vibrated to bass and the thud
of thousands dancing, drunk but nothing scary, no-one

looking for a fight. Those who had gone too far, too early,
just lay down, watched over by kind and laughing friends.

In a café decorated retro-sixties style, I ordered slices
of bread and cheese, noted the ripeness of tomatoes,

the attention to detail. Of course, in the museum quarter
life is not raw but in the park there were some paths

I thought twice about before taking, some bleary souls,
the sort I'm used to in my own chaotic ends. I expected it

to be more expensive, the day-to-day, expected to be just
politely and efficiently serviced. It was a nice surprise.

I ate chicken in apple sauce. I don't know if that's typical.
Near the Montessori school, a double-fronted shop displayed

superior taxidermy: a small big cat, a hawk dangling
a mouse by the tail, otters. Next day, I was ferried to tulips,

stood dazzled, not knowing which way to go first. I slept
in a room that was bland, white towels. It was a relief to be

a consumer of art, tulips, stroopwafel, covetable domestic
architecture. The tulips made me think it is, after all, do-able.

You Bring Out the Nottingham in Me

after Sandra Cisneros

You bring out the Hyson Green and Forest Fields
of me, Saturday night and Sunday morning love
bite signalled by a chiffon scarf.

My scent is *Dangerous October*, hot engine oil,
hot sugar, Mouse Town must. In electric dark
beyond the caravans, I take on all just

for the glory and floor them tenderly to rock n' roll,
chain and lever growl and lovely screams.
I am all these: china saucers of acetic

mushy peas, pomegranate pips eased
out with pins, bows and arrows, bouncing
fairy dolls and cocks on sticks.

Lace cuffs and stockings catch and run as Ludd
spills out of me. Only with you I'm dun sandstone,
tunnels undermine me secretly.

You bring it out of me, me duck, you do, that mardy
Lawrence fuck. With you I'm Clough-strut right, so say it,
say I walk in beauty like a Goose Fair night.

Practising being present

I comfort myself reading *minutes open into parachutes*
that fall again and fall again when, at this very minute,

a blackbird who's been fossicking among plant pots
flies up to perch, lets loose his song, insouciant, easy.

Simultaneously, from the road there's a roaring wall,
an indecipherable to-do of shout and counter-shout

as a righteous protest tangles with the flesh and gears
of the World Naked Bike Ride. The song fills the bird,

each phrase lifting a feathered ridge across his back.
He sings, 'Delicious, oh delicious beetles, all mine.'

I could be making too much of this minute, like the time
you sent a shoebox of lilies-of-the-valley from home,

filling my kitchen with the sweet viscosity of mum-love.
Flitting further up, he wipes soil off his beak and is away.

[*Quotation from Ellery Akers' 'What I do']

59

All the Way Here

Bobbers Mill

She hears me falling out of bed at night.
I play in her chip shop, spoiling paper bags
with nutty slack drenched in brown vinegar.

In our good room, the vent doll watches me.
His is a long game, square-toothed, apple-cheeked.
Calypso hisses from a liquorice disc.

Wensleydale Road

Nextdoors are sad they have no boys or girls.
I mustn't whisper through their letterbox,
I will not taste their pears or gooseberries.

Passing by poppies, I hold in my breath
in case the black dust magics me to sleep.
Spells haunt me like the maggoty dead cat.

The Ring Road

As giant fairground rides heave out of town
and whistling soldiers pass in tented trucks,
I grow ooh la la on the boulevard.

I dress to *Fun, Fun, Fun* but am happiest
lingering by the Sambre-Oise Canal,
sticky with grief for all those dear dead boys.

Blackboy Road

I just stop going in the garden when
the drains block, sleep on the floor, can barely
drag myself upright, needing less murky

'rough', fewer ley lines, paisley lies, needing
a real brown gravy dinner. I never do find out
who stole the chicken from the fridge.

Bedfordbury

Downstairs the man berates his child-like bride,
the walls are thick, the letterboxes brass.
Each night the Irish sisters fetch the police.

I hang out the window to watch Nureyev,
already dying, exit the stage door,
step from darkness into the floodlit street.

Things to Do in Small Spaces

Insinuate your tongue into
a wentletrap. Sever at the root.
Sacrifice words to make a snail.

Enter the photo booth.
Compose your face.
Try not to look like a terrorist.

Between an inner and an outer door,
here you may rest your hot head
against a wall and weep.

In a nutshell, use the time
to whittle your elbows.
Use your elbows to crack it.

Out with the Girls

We sit in the middle row,
not at the front where the film
will slap us round the face,
not at the back where we might
lose our shoes in the dark.

We talk through the adverts.
Paddy says, 'Don't you find death
becomes more attractive
the more incomprehensible
life gets?' No-one sits next to us.

Perhaps they think we'll unwrap
egg sandwiches. It's about redemption.
We distrust happy endings
though we all wear lipstick
and Jane's earrings are sensational.

What Matters

I'm watching three women sat opposite on the tube,
in rational shoes, suitably dressed for the weather,
on that familiar branch of love that has no fanfares.

I've little passion to speak of, at least not one that burns
so others might catch alight, embrace a glamorous fire,
but here I want to praise the quiet joy of old friendships,

their commonplace perfection. As a child, the sickbed treat
was mandarin oranges from a tin, evaporated milk purling
extravagantly in the juice, but always bread and butter,

steady, like these friendships' antidote to the Fancy Dan
of hectic romance or muddy-watered family ties,
each with their own complicated tendency to curdle.

The women chat – museums, books – fill in memory lapses,
supply elusive words, just now, in fact, *death mask*, their tact
so graceful it gives me comfort. They say so much

but what matters is their voices' easy harmony, accomplished
in this way of friendship as a Mozart trio carried by singers
at the peak of their art, having practiced over all these years.

What I learnt behind bars

The Manvers Arms

I never saw the exotic dancer's snake,
being deemed too green for the hurly-burly
of the public bar and consigned upstairs

to the lounge, to ferry steaks au poivre
and cherries jubilee from the echoing kitchen
where a solitary boy in whites dropped

plastic sachets into water at a rolling boil
and gave up trying before he'd even started.
To a woman, the lady diners despised me

in my pink satin hot pants with the butterfly
appliqué. They were right. It wasn't a uniform,
nobody made me wear them but I had the legs.

The Flying Horse

I was filling in the rest of that last summer
when those Aussie lads we'd met
on the Piazzale Michelangelo
during the earth tremor
took us at our word,

hopped over to England and popped by.
It was several years until I came to see
that when the tidy men in the intimate bar
by the door had sighed I was lucky,
it hadn't been on account of my fabulous tan

or hair so straight it didn't need ironing
but because of those ragamuffin boys
who swept in and swept me up
in their loud glory, lighting every corner
with their shameless brio.

The Dover Castle

A solicitor called Christian owned the Dover Castle
and lived above with his largely incidental wife
who rose at six to make miniature shepherd's pies.

He had another round the corner but, it was agreed,
the Castle was the classier. By noon it was full
of doctors and the BBC drinking vodka and tonic.

On hot days he'd turn off the pumps and offer
only continental bottled beers to quench the thirst
of consultants, commissioning editors and engineers

sweating in the mews. If we had cucumbers,
he'd make up a jug of Pimm's. In the afternoons
we bottled up, counted pennies from the machines

and Mitti would rail against the gracelessness
of English men. Of an evening it was quiet,
just regulars: a psychiatrist from Harley Street,

who specialised in Catholic guilt, drank
until he liquefied, and the man in the stetson
practiced being inscrutable over Jack Daniels.

Tipster Laurie, fresh from the courses, in thrall
to hard-hearted Mitti, could be coaxed into sending
a taxi for ice-cream as the dullness wore on,

soaked in scotches drawn from six optics, all filled
from the big bargain bottle. When David Warner,
in his Morgan years, sat on the step, head in hands,

I offered him the solace of the poster for his Hamlet
which had graced my teenage wall and agreed
that neither of us should be here. A man who said

he'd designed the packaging for Winalot invited me
to late supper at the Hard Rock Café and I went.
It seemed starry but really it was just sticky carpet work.

Short-lifers in The Bury

And here were the people somehow left behind,
who hadn't made it yet to Wild Street's sumptuous
bathrooms and electricity, who lacked the push,
that sure vocabulary of rights, to get themselves

decanted before we arrived – our careless caravan
of bean bags, marijuana and home-brew kits –
allowed to occupy the voids pending demolition.
A lav on the landing was small price for the chance

to play house at a peppercorn behind the Coliseum,
where Dickens lingered in the old photographer's
yellow vulpine smile, in the three slim sisters'
identical chignons, in the pantomime-costumed

bell-hop who beat his wife. These left-behind
– box office, porters, messengers for the Inns –
past the time of employment, edged warily round
us gong-voiced incomers who knew nothing

of Brasso, of turn and turnabout, who echoed all hours
in the corridors, colonising the cubbyhole bathroom
with our profligate steam, the air with our rootless music,
mislaid the keys, were there and then were gone.

Ash Priors

I don't remember the season. The cottage was dour
and damp even in summer: small fire in a vast hearth,

the mantelpiece ranged with pewter plates and knights
but the chimney wouldn't draw and flour in the pantry

was mobile with weevils. Ripe goat skin rug, a settle,
six oak chairs and not one offering any ordinary ease.

And those waits, not knowing if a bus was due that hour,
that day, that week, snails having eaten the timetable.

Hidden from the road, its very name a poem, the place
added to your doleful charm, orphaned, irresistible

and me from next door to a chip shop, just learning
to walk hobbled by my long brown velveteen skirt.

We were living on myths and tea in the ragtag end
of an all-going-wrong, went nights without sleep

then baked our hennaed heads in the sun, green mud
staining our fingers ochre. You and your friend

were playing Risk again and I was reading someone's
'Hawk in the Rain', when there it was, now and now,

entering the dark hole of my head. It was then, well,
let's say it was then, that I knew I would be alright.

Me and Keats on the Heath

We're late for sloes, the lower branches cleared,
so we have to push into nettles, jump up to catch
then bend down the tops to get at the good fruits,
like small damsons, with that same midnight bloom.

Some say to wait for frost to split the skins, others
to patiently prick each berry so the juice will ooze.
Some say half a kilo but I've found just a handful
can achieve the desired conundrum: is it good?

Or does it taste like medicine? Those three beeches
were only saplings in your time, John, out of bounds
in a private estate. Now they're public and anyone
may picnic under them. Even noise has changed.

You'd know that soughing of the leaves but not
the press of planes or the high shush of fast bikes.
We leave the brambles, too mean compared with
the cultivars I've already set steeping in cheap vodka.

We know we don't have the knowledge for fungi,
fear blundering into a lurid death, but we admire
their blooming, yellow and orange on fallen trees.
The new lake is settling in, nicely fringed with sedges.

Apple Day: An Apology

The air thins. I stand underneath the trees,
contrite, my hand held up to cup and test
with reverential twist your readiness
to drop into my waiting palm. And yes,

all this forgetful summer passed away
I've dallied with the long-haul charlatans,
swallowed their false promise shamefully,
their brief sweetness ashes on my tongue.

Blame my impatience, my green eagerness
for your vinaceous strawberry hit, for nut
unfolding under your respective flush
of crimson, your chafed cheek rusticoat.

The day's edge narrows into true autumn.
You hang, a gathering of light. Is it time?

On the Difficulty of Working with Quinces

Lacking deftness, knowledge
of knots, an extra hand,
I fumble the gathering-up,

allow the muslin swell
to press against the bowl,
releasing cloudiness

from the yellow collapse
so the slow drops coalesce
to perfumed milky pink.

My jars will hum not sing
like those of the truly adept.
Theirs are jars of the mythic

larder with the high window
fitted with fine mesh,
shallow shelves, marble slab,

where I could spend days
rearranging oyster sauce
and mace, cups of solid fat

concealing savoury grit,
Red Leicester in greaseproof,
celery like a bouquet in a jug.

All there is to know about jam

Do you have neighbours with a glut or a mate
who smells of bonfire? Either way, the fruit
will need rinsing, picking over for woodlice,
stems and bruises. Then lug out that heavy pan

from behind the madeleine trays. You must
break down the fruit before adding sugar,
less than they say. Slowly, stirring through
resistance, melt the sugar from grit to syrup

then turn up the heat to a hell. The faster you
reach setting point, the brighter the jewel.
You might flinch from the spatter. Don't leave.
Scum surfaces. Skim it. Now, drag off the heat

to test by wrinkle or use a thermometer scaled
from Yoghurt to Crack. Sniff out any pickle taint
in the hot jars you've lined up then fill to the lip.
Whack on lids and label in your neatest writing.

That's it, but be prepared to find that, cold, it may
turn out you jumped the gun, have sauce, or dithered
and it's solid, destined for years on a shelf until,
brushing away mouse droppings, you finally bin it.

Downstairs at the LRB bookshop with the older women poets

For Mimi

This afternoon we women create without even trying
an invisible electrical fence which deters the would-be
customer in the Poetry Section. They've given us a table.
Below, our feet in comfy shoes, above, the ta-ran-ta-ra

of scarves and witty jewellery. The table's set with glasses,
napkins, water for those on tablets, and small treats: wine,
fat salted cashews, cordial made from the berries of the tree
said to repel or be a meeting place for hags. We're here

to hear our poet spin gold. She says she's close to early Vuillard.
His studio, his mother's workroom, wallpaper, soft furnishings
and the figures in what is usually thought of as foreground
are all of a piece, of equal status. Memory and connections

manifest in a wine glass, an etui, in a mille fiore print.
She says her many solitary café hours could pass for idleness,
but we're not fooled a bit. True teachers are holy after all
and should be borne on palanquins. I'd thought of bringing

an offering of quince jelly but didn't, worried even a small jar
might be a burden. I make do with jam talk with the girl
from the upstairs café who, half way through, serves us
almond cake, dense and damp with bitter marmalade.

Books surround us. Perhaps we're dry but dry as kindling,
ready to catch light. Our poet says she's not interested in story,
what it's about or not, what it might mean, rather, she prizes
that grape, Woolf's yellowy grape of a juicy moment.

Penguin Modern Poets 10, 1967

It's like that very first episode of *Corrie* when suddenly
here are people we know. The point is we are young,
not in London and not about to die of shrapnel or TB.

We're outside but in earshot of someone's flagging party,
bored, bone-tired, fingers stained with the boiled beetroot
of a Saturday job, past drunk and wanting a sandwich,

no idea of how we're going to get home. Then the moon rises
and hangs over an ornamental fishpond. Tell me how to be
unfathomable, not just one of your too frequent schoolgirls.

You're alive, walking similar streets. I need you to tell me
I'm interesting, notice my gloves, my peculiar fishing habits.
I need you to crash through bay windows, give me leave.

Calligraphy Blues

I feel I need another hand, one whose glyphs
and gestures waft sentiment with the insouciance
of a silk peignoir or the scarf that did for Isadora,
redolent of bergamot rather than wet English Setter,
or hard-buttoned gabardine, one with long sillage,
in a tongue that reads another way. If I could write
as though hovering between line and heaven,
drop with the grace and hunger of a goshawk,
phantom of the forest, or a falcon snatching life
out of the air, I could, I think, outrun the idiolect
which binds me, makes me so rational, so carefully
ironic in Linked Script, its three set heights above
the line, one full depth below; so very, very legible.

Mercy

I dream forgetfully, retain just a suggestion
of something thwarted. My husband dreams

of murder, all hands-on: noose, bludgeon,
knives. He's under orders to kill, demurs,

he says, in vain. This is a man who dispatches
prolapsed chickens, mice, once a muntjac fawn

half-garrotted on a wire fence, a man who salts
ox tongue, the great muscle sitting outside

five days in a big pan, covered against snow
and crows. If I remember a dream, it's sludgy,

like running against an ebbing tide. Awake,
I'd turn, give in, fall back onto the drag.

I'm no fighter. It was so small, the fawn,
he said, he thought it was a cub. It was only

when its mother waded upstream he realised
what it was, *had been*. I dream of journeys

which end in no place much, hours to wait
until the next bus back. Sometimes the feeling

doesn't match the story, leaks out into the day.
I seldom wake up crying, less than once a year.

Music & Movement

We're in our knickers, hungry as always.
Some of us are vestless but it's no disgrace,

it's months before we'll learn to be mortified
by nipples. After marching, we're divided:

tree-girls, static, arms aloft, and wind-boys
who career – hurricanes, tornados – oblivious

to the radio. Branches spread high and wide,
we trees persist in our valiant waving despite

the idiot winds' rude buffetings which knock us
sideways. I am silver birch, arboreally furious,

white-trunked in spotless cotton interlock.
My fringe is an owl, my beetle brows a hawk,

all murderous attention as twig fingers stir
and test the unsuspecting mouse-flavoured air.

My legs, my legs are mighty. No callow gusts
will better me. Each copse, each wood, each forest

will roar when I am wind, every single tree.
When I get to be wind, I'll do it properly.

ACKNOWLEDGEMENTS

Some of the poems in this collection or versions of them were first published by The Emma Press, Fenland Reed, And Other Poems, Brittle Star, The Rialto, London Grip, The North, Magma, 14, Under the Radar, Smith Doorstop, Live Canon, Poem, Finished Creatures, Poetry Archive Now! Wordview 2020, South Bank Poetry, Mslexia and Morning Star.

My heartfelt thanks go to the incomparable Mimi Khalvati, to Ann and Peter Sansom, to Richard Price and to the talented, challenging and generous groups of poets they gather round them. To Stuart Bartholomew and Emma Dai'an Wright for taking a chance on me. To artist and friend Sharon Smart for the beautiful cover illustration. And last but not least to Ramona Herdman, Fokkina McDonnell, Sarah Mnatzaganian, Paul Stephenson and Pam Thompson who have kept me on the poetry lifeboat through the storms of the last couple of years.

ABOUT VERVE POETRY PRESS

Verve Poetry Press is a quite new and already prize-winning press that focused initially on meeting a local need in Birmingham - a need for the vibrant poetry scene here in Brum to find a way to present itself to the poetry world via publication. Co-founded by Stuart Bartholomew and Amerah Saleh, it now publishes poets from all corners of the UK - poets that speak to the city's varied and energetic qualities and will contribute to its many poetic stories.

Added to this is a colourful pamphlet series, many featuring poets who have performed at our sister festival - and a poetry show series which captures the magic of longer poetry performance pieces by festival alumni such as Polarbear, Matt Abbott and Imogen Stirling.

The press has been voted Most Innovative Publisher at the Saboteur Awards, and has won the Publisher's Award for Poetry Pamphlets at the Michael Marks Awards.

Like the festival, we strive to think about poetry in inclusive ways and embrace the multiplicity of approaches towards this glorious art.

www.vervepoetrypress.com
@VervePoetryPres
mail@vervepoetrypress.com